A Few Feral Fables
Volume 1

Written and Lived by
Lora Hardin

A Few Feral Fables: Volume 1
by Lora Hardin
Includes:
The Methed-Up Raccoon and the Dumpster Fire
LaQueefa: The Elephant with Amnesia
Anal the Alcoholic Armadillo
A Feral Manifesto
I wish, I wish

For inquiries, permissions, or further information, contact:
Lora Hardin
All Feral Fables Press

First Edition – 2025

To my mom:
who has always done what she could

To my sponsor:
who has never given up on me, despite my chronic insanity

To my therapist:
who has helped me to find my voice, wherever the fuck I put it at

The Methed-Up Raccoon and the Dumpster Fire

Once upon a time, there was a raccoon who lived in a dumpster behind a grocery store. She didn't choose it. It was more like a situation where life had shoved her there, so this is just what she's doing now. It wasn't glamorous (unless you like half-eaten bologna sandwiches), but it was hers.

The other raccoons said that she was
too much, or not enough.
Too loud.
Too quiet.
Too stubborn.
Too passive.

So she stayed in her dumpster, half hiding, half hoping someone might notice that she was worth something.

When she was just a small raccoon, she was told that she was stupid, fat, worthless. She was shown hatred and violence. She learned that “love” came with teeth and claws and fear.

She carried those wounds deep inside her, where no one could see them, but they itched and burned all the same, like fleas on her soul.

As an adult, she tried to make herself "just enough." She became the cleverest dumpster diver, the quietest when needed, the loudest when required. She even tried the game of marriage, thinking that maybe if she played it just right, that she would finally belong to someone.

Spoiler alert: she did not belong.

That game had rules that she never got to write.

And when her little raccoon daughter and her little raccoon stepson were taken from her paws, she felt smaller than ever. She felt like a background character in her own story.

Then came the meth. At first, it was fun, a trick to silence the noise in her mind. But soon, the meth was out of control. Her dumpster was not a home anymore. It was a full-blown fucking dumpster fire. It was the kind that you could see blocks away, lighting up the night sky with smoke, sparks, and bad life choices. She nearly burned herself to death many times.

And yet, when the flames died down, something fucking weird happened. From the ashes, she crawled out, singed whiskers and all. She didn't even feel like a raccoon anymore, just a hollow, crispy shell of what once was.

But she found that she wasn't alone. There was something bigger than her. Call it the Moon, or a Dump Truck, or simply a Power greater than one tiny raccoon with garbage breath.

That Power whispered:

You don't have to live in the dumpster anymore.
You can walk.
You can have freedom.
You can have peace.

So she left behind that dumpster. She also left behind her fears:

Fear of being too much or too little.

Fear of failing.

Fear of being seen.

She walked forward, one cautious paw at a time. She learned to carry gratitude for every scar, every flame, every flea bite because each one had shaped her into the raccoon who could now walk, and no longer had to crawl.

And though she still sometimes tripped over her own tail, she began to trust herself. She knew deep down in her flea-bitten soul that she was capable. She knew that even in her worst struggles, she had always kept moving.

And that was exactly enough.

And so the raccoon walked on — not toward perfection or applause, but toward life itself.

Because sometimes, the bravest thing that a methed-up raccoon can do is climb out of her own dumpster fire, shake off the ashes, and limp forward - teeth bared, eyes open, and fucking alive.

LaQueefa:
The Elephant with Amnesia

Once upon a time, there was an elephant who was terrible at being an elephant. Everyone said elephants never forget. This one forgot pretty much everything.

Her storybook wasn't just missing a page or two, whole sections were hacked out with rusty scissors. She could recall the pain of her father's tusks, the sting of never belonging, the way that she learned to shrink herself into something small and unnoticeable. But the good stuff? The soft stuff? That was the first to get wiped. Because apparently trauma comes with a lifetime warranty, but joy has an expiration date.

Her daughter's first steps... gone. The one milestone that should've been tattooed on her mama brain in neon ink. Erased like chalk in the rain.

The memories of her brother, not only as kids but as adults stumbling through life together? They had vacated the premises. A whole relationship flattened into static.

Coworkers that she had spent 5, 10, 15 years with? They might as well have been extras in someone else's movie. Sometimes she would meet them later in life and it was always like meeting strangers.

Her childhood best friend, who deserved better than an early death and deserved more than being forgotten by someone who loved her so much. She was now just an outline of a ghost that she cannot sharpen no matter how hard she tries.

And her grandfather's final years, the man who called her Cricket, loved her like no one else, and inspired her love of music? Erased. Skipped like someone hit fast-forward through the most important scenes.

And of course, other elephants liked to "helpfully" remind her: “Remember when you said this?” or “Remember when we did that?” She’d plaster on a smile, maybe nod, while inside her chest cracked like thin ice. No, she didn’t fucking remember. She hated that. And she hated herself for pretending. It felt like stealing someone else’s life and signing her name at the bottom.

Grief came in waves. Not just grief for the people she'd lost, but grief for losing them twice: once when life took them, and again when her brain deleted them. That's a special kind of cruelty. It's like a thief that steals what you had and then steals the proof that it ever even existed.

Still, she kept walking. Because what the hell else could she do? Lie down in the mud and rot?

So she made new steps. Heavy, deliberate, and usually sarcastic as hell but forward all the same. Each step gave her a chance to discover something unfiltered, something that was hers. And here's the twist: she wasn't just rebuilding her memory, she was rebuilding her self. What smells did she like? What adventures? What sounds? She didn't know. Some days she caught herself wondering if she was rediscovering old favorites or trying on something brand-new. Either way, it was hers now.

One day it was the smell of baby soap. Another day it was a song. And again the sound of her own queef, this one she couldn't forget this time, not if she could help it. Every little discovery was like planting a flag in unknown territory: *Mine. This is mine now.*

Yes, her library was burned. Yes, the ghosts of lost memories trailed her like a bad smell. But she wasn't stagnant. She was still coloring, still experimenting, still living. Every step forward gave her the chance to stack new memories beside the ashes of the old, and to shape a self she could actually recognize, even if it changed every day.

She would never stop grieving the losses: her stepson's laugh, her best friend's warmth, her daughter's firsts that she never got to keep. That pain would never scrub out. And she carried another fear like a stone in her stomach: *what if she kept losing more?* What if her mind kept flickering until even today's flags in the ground got ripped up? That thought sometimes paralyzed her. But sometimes, it pushed her to keep building anyway. If the future meant more obliteration, then she'd damn well outpace them with more memories.

She was deeply grateful for every picture and video she had of her daughter, stepson, past pets, family, and friends. Sometimes she didn't know if she remembered the actual moment, or just the picture. The timeline in her head was confusing and full of fear while the camera roll told a different story. That disconnect was disturbing, confusing, sometimes unbearable. But still, she was grateful, because at least there was proof. Proof that she had lived those days, even if her brain had locked those doors.

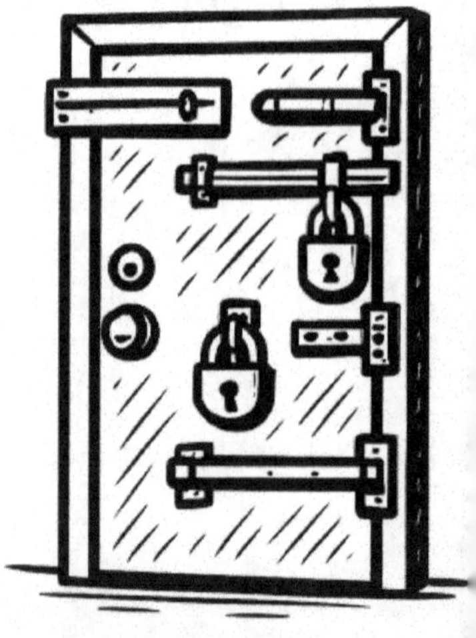

And so the elephant gave herself a new name: LaQueefa. A little ridiculous, a little insolent, but absolutely hers. She might forget birthdays, milestones, whole years. But she would not forget who she was becoming. Because if her memory was going to betray her, at least her queef wouldn't.

She can now say to herself: Fine. Those memories are gone. I'll keep them as ghosts. But I'll make more. Better ones. And they'll be mine. Me. LaQueefa. Whoever the hell that is today.

And for an elephant who wasn’t supposed to forget, that was more than enough.

Anal the Alcoholic Armadillo

Once upon a time, there was an armadillo named Anal. On the outside she looked tough with her shiny shell. On the inside, she was full of chaos.

Growing up, her armadillo dad had words and claws that were mean and sharp, so she learned early to curl up tight and roll away.

In college she rolled straight into a drunken rampage. The spinning didn't stop, and she failed out after just one semester. So she marched into the military life instead. There she learned order and how to pack her mess down tight, but the chaos inside her shell never actually stopped, no matter how much she drank.

She married a mean armadillo man. She had a cute armadillo daughter. For a while that little girl gave her a reason to peek her head out. But when the marriage cracked, the bottle and resentment towards the world and her own self slid right in and unpacked its fucking bags. Anal rolled deeper and deeper into misery until she lost her daughter.

She tried to stop many times. She tried every trick, every bargain, every promise. Nothing worked, not even a trip to Disney Land.

She even tried to roll herself right out of this world more than once, but traffic always seemed to somehow miss this particular armadillo. She had tried to roll herself so many times that she was convinced that she was either immortal or really fucking stupid. But she always woke up; hungover, still trapped inside the same shell, still hating herself and the world around her.

One day Anal rolled into a room that she never wanted to be in: an AA meeting. The chairs were plain. The sayings were fucking stupid. But the people there knew her story without her even saying a single word.

So, she got a sponsor. She was handed a life map called "the 12 Steps." She tried talking to something bigger than her shell; a Higher Power who could stand between her and the bottle. And soon after she reached out, He whispered back: "*You don't have to live in that shell anymore. You can have freedom. You can have peace.*"

For a while she tasted that peace, and the air inside her armor felt lighter. Then she slipped. Not back into the bottle, but into another shiny trap. Another addiction. Another fucking mess. She tried to stop that, too, and could not do it by herself.

So finally, on her knees, knees that hadn't seen this much action since college, she prayed. Every time she wanted to use, she hit the floor or the gravel or even stealing a moment behind a portapotty. She asked her Higher Power to stand between her and that addiction. To take away the want once again. Day after day, knees sore and shell bruised, she asked.

And something shifted. The grip loosened. The chaos quieted. Today, Anal still has her shell. She still knows how to roll. But she also still has a relationship with a Higher Power, she's working the Steps again, and she still has a sponsor who tells her the fucking truth when she doesn't want to fucking hear it. She is showing up and being present in her relationships.

The peace that she has found so far isn't fireworks. It's breathing room. It's being able to fall asleep without negotiating with herself first. It's laughing a little louder and a little longer. It's driving home and realizing that she's smiling for no fucking reason in particular. It's walking with her daughter again without dragging a bottle like a ball and chain. It's being able to adult... some days.

She still stumbles. She still forgets and thinks that she can do it alone. But she remembers those knees, remembers the way that asking felt, and she asks again each day.

Anal doesn’t claim to be fixed. But today she knows that rolling up in her shell with alcohol does not have to be her life. Today she has a choice. Today she has a sufficient substitute and a life that she doesn't hate waking up to.

A Feral Manifesto

I am not tame anymore.
I tried that once. I tried to be gentle, palatable, pleasant. I folded myself into polite silence, wore shame like perfume, and smiled until my cheeks hurt. It didn't save me.
Feral is what happens when you stop apologizing for surviving.
It's not rage. It's reclamation. It's the soft animal of me, tired of performing, stepping out of the cage with a smirk and a story.
What feral means to me:

- I laugh too loud and cry without warning.
- I love things with teeth and stories with scars.
- I don't owe you pretty, polite, or small.
- I know the rules – I just choose when they are worth following.

My healing isn't a spa day. It's a forest fire.
And when the ashes settle, I'll still be here
- barefoot, unbothered, and probably
petting something I shouldn't.
I'm not broken. I'm just feral now - and
this is the most honest I've ever been.

I Wish, I Wish

I wish, I wish your angry words were gone,
gone, gone, gone for good.

I wish, I wish it was only on T.V.

I wish, I wish I could turn down the
volume.

I wish, I wish I could keep it down until
your angry words are gone.

I wish, I wish I could keep it down until a
happy ending comes within me.

I wish, I wish your angry words were gone,
gone, gone forever.

If you or someone you know is struggling with addiction or mental health, help is out there.
You are not alone.

Call or text 988 (Suicide & Crisis Lifeline)

Veterans Crisis Line - Call or text 988 and press 1, or chat at veteranscrisisline.net

SAMHSA's National Helpline
1-800-662-HELP (4357)

Alcoholics Anonymous - aa.org

Narcotics Anonymous - na.org

National Mental Health Hotline / Crisis Text Line Text "HOME" to 741741

www.ingramcontent.com/pod-product-compliance
Lightning Source LLC
LaVergne TN
LVHW080000210926
848481LV00012B/3632